LOOK INSIDE
CROSS-SECTIONS
CARS

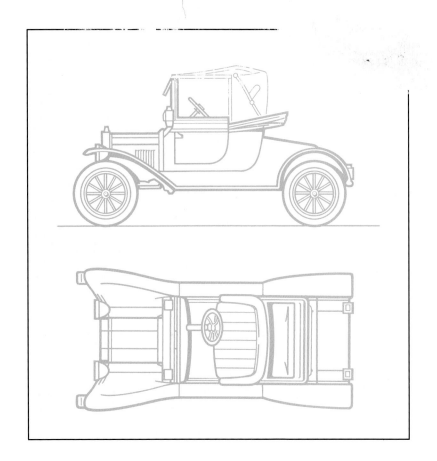

LOOK INSIDE
CROSS-SECTIONS
CARS

ILLUSTRATED BY
ALAN AUSTIN

WRITTEN BY
MICHAEL JOHNSTONE

DORLING KINDERSLEY
LONDON • NEW YORK • STUTTGART

A DORLING KINDERSLEY BOOK

Art Editor Dorian Spencer Davies
Designers Sharon Grant, Sara Hill
Senior Art Editor C. David Gillingwater
Project Editor Constance Novis
Senior Editor John C. Miles
Production Louise Barratt
Consultant Jonathan Day
The National Motor Museum, Beaulieu

First published in 1994
by Dorling Kindersley Limited,
9 Henrietta Street, London WC2E 8PS

A CIP catalogue record for this book is available
from the British Library

ISBN 0-7513-5219-5

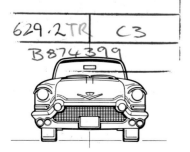

Reproduced by Dot Gradations, Essex
Printed and bound by Proost, Belgium

CONTENTS

MODEL T FORD 6-7

BENTLEY 8-9

CITROEN 10-11

WILLYS JEEP 12-13

MODEL T FORD

IN THE EARLY YEARS OF MOTORING, only the rich could afford a car. Henry Ford changed that. In 1903, he founded the Ford Motor Company and produced the Model A. It was based on the shape of a horse-drawn buggy, but with an engine under the seat! Five years later, the Model T appeared: it sold for $825. By 1927, when it went out of production, 5,007,033 "tin lizzies" had been produced and the price had fallen to $260. In 1913, Ford introduced a moving assembly line, operated by a winch. By the end of that year, Ford workers could assemble a complete car in 93 minutes. Other car manufacturers took days, even weeks, to make their cars, which meant they were much more expensive.

"Any colour they want"

Early Model Ts came in red, grey, and green. In 1914 the only paint that would dry quickly enough to keep up with the speed of the assembly line was black Japanese enamel. When Ford heard this, he said that anyone who wanted to buy a Model T could have it in any colour they wanted, "As long as it's black!"

Stopping, reversing, and speeding

To stop the car, the driver pressed down the right-hand brake pedal. To put it in reverse he put the car in neutral and then pressed down the middle pedal. The driver controlled the car's speed by pulling on a "throttle" handle.

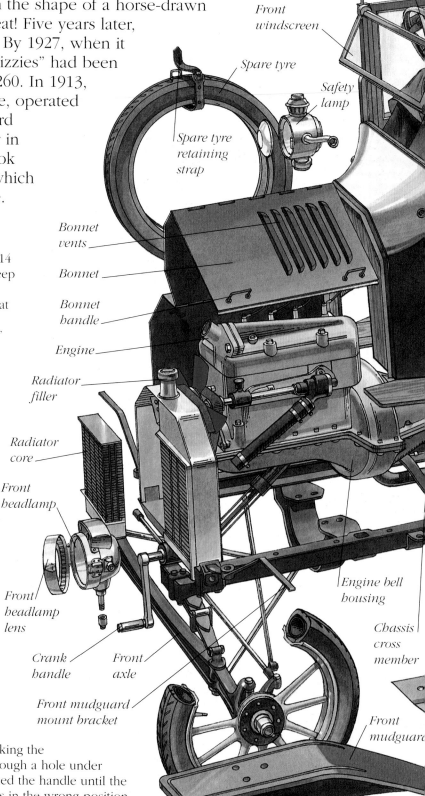

Steering wheel

Front windscreen

Spare tyre

Safety lamp

Spare tyre retaining strap

Bonnet vents

Bonnet

Bonnet handle

Engine

Radiator filler

Radiator core

Front headlamp

Front headlamp lens

Crank handle

Front axle

Front mudguard mount bracket

Engine bell housing

Chassis cross member

Front mudguard

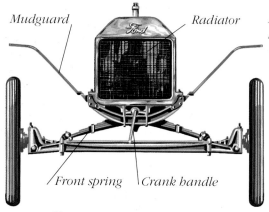

Mudguard

Radiator

Front spring

Crank handle

FRONT VIEW OF MODEL T

Getting started

Drivers of early Model Ts had to start them by cranking the engine. They fitted one end of a starting handle through a hole under the radiator leading into the engine. Then they turned the handle until the engine spluttered into life. If the ignition switch was in the wrong position the starting handle would spring back violently when the engine started, leaving many inexperienced motorists with broken arms, wrists, or thumbs!

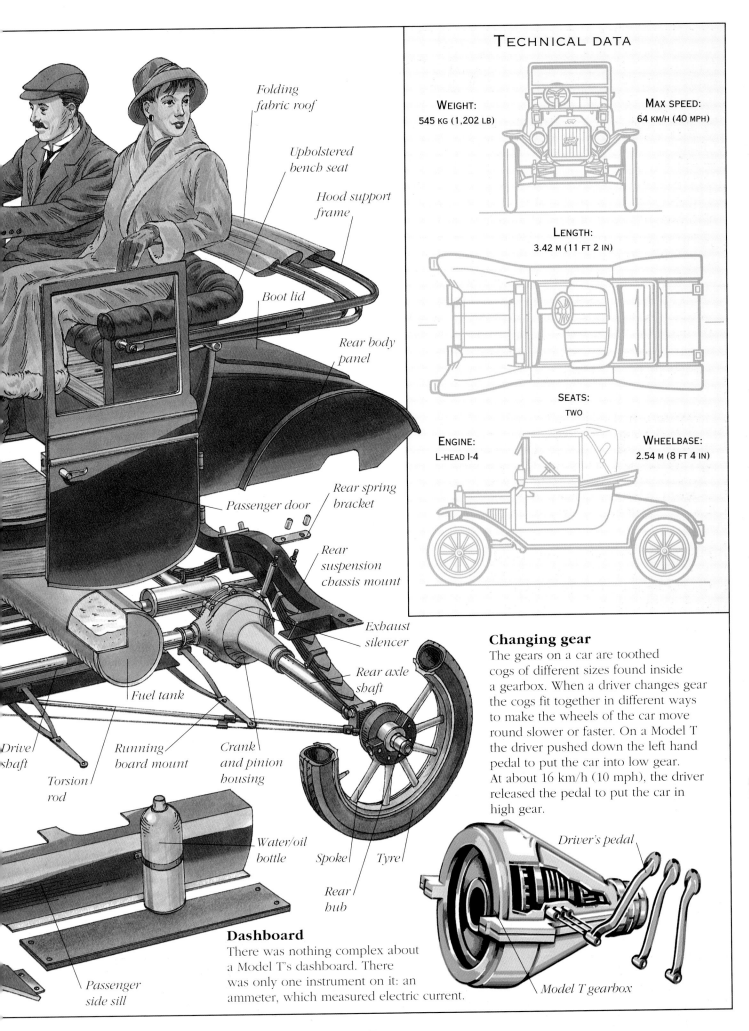

Folding fabric roof

Upholstered bench seat

Hood support frame

Boot lid

Rear body panel

Passenger door

Rear spring bracket

Rear suspension chassis mount

Exhaust silencer

Rear axle shaft

Drive shaft

Torsion rod

Running board mount

Fuel tank

Crank and pinion housing

Water/oil bottle

Spoke

Tyre

Rear hub

Passenger side sill

Changing gear

The gears on a car are toothed cogs of different sizes found inside a gearbox. When a driver changes gear the cogs fit together in different ways to make the wheels of the car move round slower or faster. On a Model T the driver pushed down the left hand pedal to put the car into low gear. At about 16 km/h (10 mph), the driver released the pedal to put the car in high gear.

Driver's pedal

Model T gearbox

Dashboard

There was nothing complex about a Model T's dashboard. There was only one instrument on it: an ammeter, which measured electric current.

BENTLEY

EARLY IN THE DEVELOPMENT OF THE CAR, enthusiasts found a way of increasing the power of the engine. The device used to do this was called a supercharger. Superchargers, or "blowers", were first used in the mid-1920s. Bentley cars were first supercharged after 1928 when Sir Henry "Tim" Birkin, driving a standard Bentley, finished in eighth place in a race in Germany. He approached an engineer called Amherst Villiers to design the supercharger. Although only a handful of Bentley Blowers were built, they have become, in the eyes of many, the most sought-after motor cars in the world.

SUPERCHARGER DETAILS

Rotor

Casing

Drive shaft

Bearing housing

End casing

Power booster
Superchargers use rotating vanes to enrich the air/petrol mix in each cylinder and boost the engine's power. The Bentley's supercharger was right at the front, between the headlamps.

Bonnet

Inspection panel

Air vent

Engine cowling strap

Radiator filler cap

Engine head

All about engines
The engine of a car provides power by mixing petrol with air and burning the mixture in the engine cylinders. The gases produced expand rapidly, pushing down pistons that turn the crankshaft and wheels.

Front mudguard

Front headlamp

Headlamp lens grille

Twin carburettors

Supercharger

Wheel spoke

Ignition coil

Steering arm

Sump filler cap

Bonnet sill

Starter motor

Footwell

Exhaust manifold

Tyre

The chassis
The chassis of a car is the metal frame, wheels, engine, and mechanical parts attached to the body. Bentley did not supply the bodies, called the "coachwork", for their cars.

Front wheel spin off

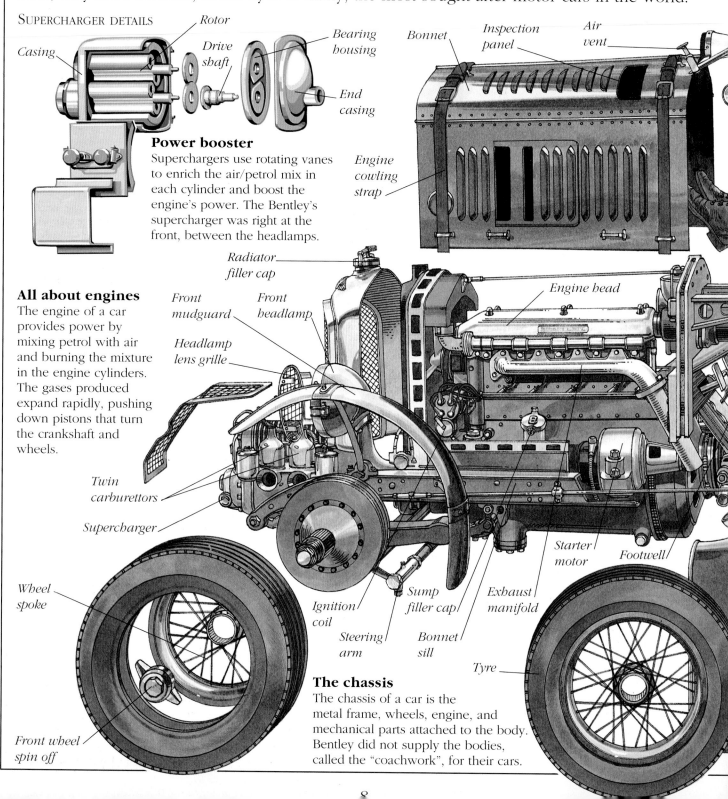

he dashboard

he dashboard in the Blower was made of aluminium
nd housed more instruments than many aircraft of the
ay. There was no standard layout, but in most models
e speedometer was just to the left of the steering wheel.
he fuel gauge was alongside it to the left, just below
e tachometer. This showed the driver at a glance
ow hard the engine was working by counting the revs.

Aero
screen

Racing
goggles

Cork
helmet

Steering
wheel

Driver's
seat

Folding
roof

Gear
lever

Handbrake

ckpit
cia

Fuel
tank
filler

On the road

The rules of the Le Mans, the
24-hour race held every year in
France, said that at least 50
examples of any model in the
competition must be offered
for sale to the public.
Bentley therefore made 50
production cars as well as
the racing models.

Rear
mesh

Rear
lamp

Fuel
tank

Drive shaft
coupling

Floor
panel

Link
arm

Linkage rod

Passenger
door

Rear
differential

Rear
coach
spring

Rear suspension
damper

Rear axle
spline

Rear brake
drum

"Corrupt"

Walter O. Bentley, the man who founded the firm, did not
want his cars supercharged. "To supercharge a Bentley,"
he said, "is to corrupt its performance." Even before the
Blower was on the road, the Bentley company was in
financial trouble. In 1931 it was taken over by Rolls-Royce.

CITROEN

IN 1932, FRENCH CAR-MAKER André Citroën announced that he would build a strong, light car with some very innovative features. Within eighteen months he was true to his word and the first *Traction Avant*, the "A-series" 7cv, appeared on the road. His great achievement was to produce a car with up-to-the-minute engineering at a price that ordinary people could afford. He died almost bankrupt in 1935, but his *Traction Avant* stayed in production in various models until 1957. Even today there are still some on the road, cherished by their fortunate owners.

Pulling from the front

Citroën decided that his car would have front-wheel drive – the car is pulled along by the front wheels as opposed to being pushed along by the rear ones. Hence the name: *Traction Avant*, French for "pulling front".

Styled for ewe

Early Citroën advertising showed how, with its flat floor, the *Traction Avant* could be used to transport animals such as sheep in the back.

Keeping things level

Suspension systems keep a car's wheels on the road and protect passengers from being shaken too much. Early cars had simple springs to absorb the shock. The *Traction Avant* was fitted with bars called torsion bars, which acted as springs.

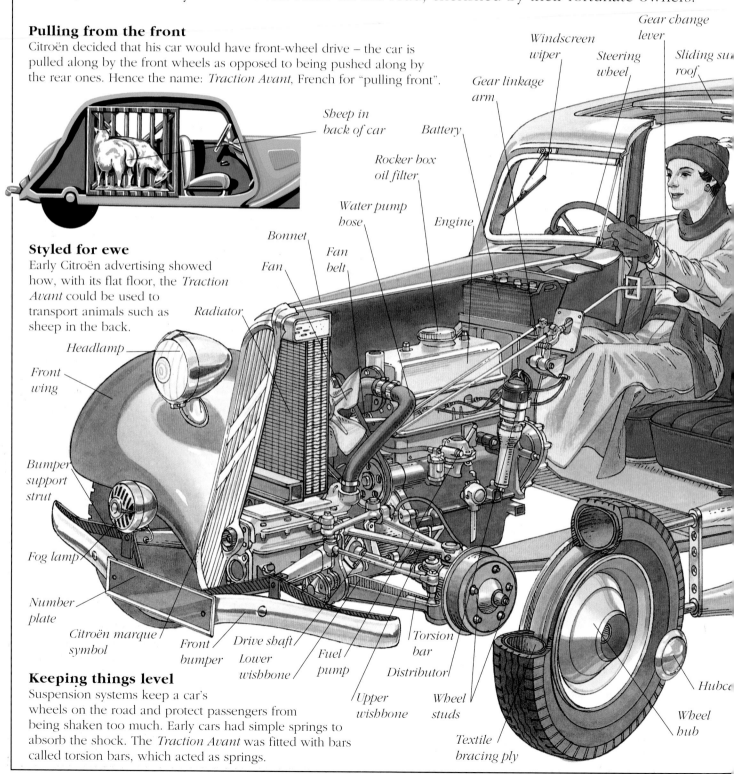

Sheep in back of car

Gear change lever

Windscreen wiper

Steering wheel

Sliding sun roof

Gear linkage arm

Battery

Rocker box oil filter

Water pump hose

Engine

Bonnet

Fan belt

Fan

Radiator

Headlamp

Front wing

Bumper support strut

Fog lamp

Number plate

Citroën marque symbol

Front bumper

Drive shaft

Lower wishbone

Fuel pump

Upper wishbone

Torsion bar

Distributor

Wheel studs

Hubca

Wheel hub

Textile bracing ply

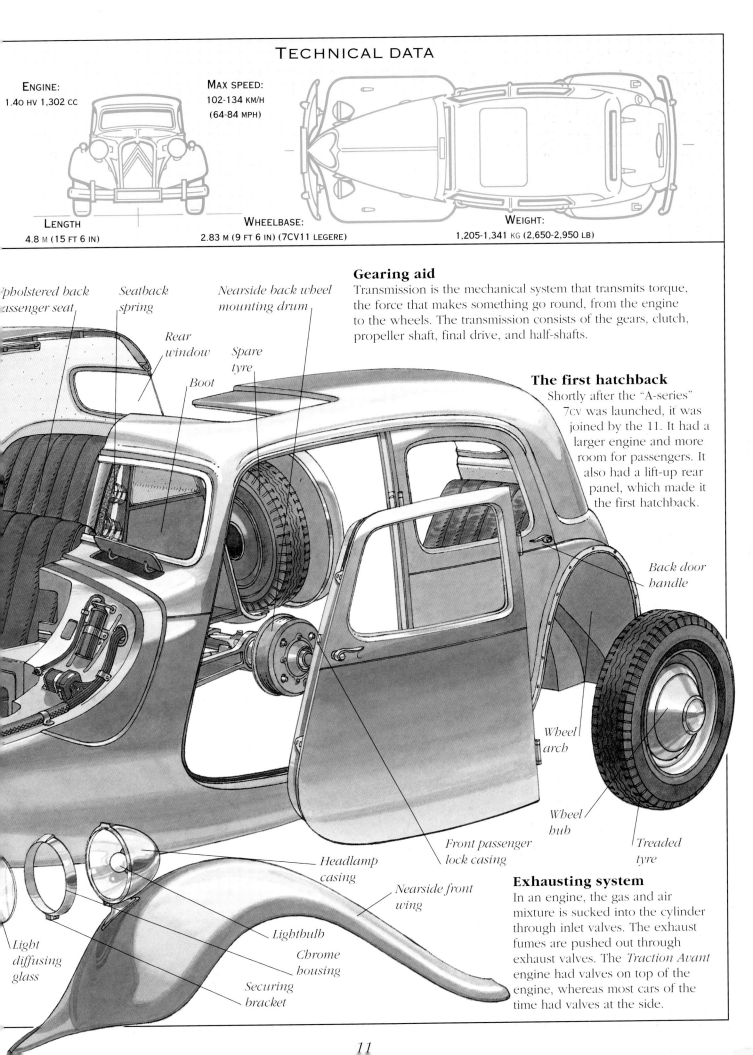

ENGINE:
1.4O HV 1,302 CC

MAX SPEED:
102-134 KM/H
(64-84 MPH)

LENGTH
4.8 M (15 FT 6 IN)

WHEELBASE:
2.83 M (9 FT 6 IN) (7CV11 LEGERE)

WEIGHT:
1,205-1,341 KG (2,650-2,950 LB)

Upholstered back
passenger seat

Seatback
spring

Nearside back wheel
mounting drum

Rear
window

Spare
tyre

Boot

Gearing aid

Transmission is the mechanical system that transmits torque, the force that makes something go round, from the engine to the wheels. The transmission consists of the gears, clutch, propeller shaft, final drive, and half-shafts.

The first hatchback

Shortly after the "A-series" 7cv was launched, it was joined by the 11. It had a larger engine and more room for passengers. It also had a lift-up rear panel, which made it the first hatchback.

Back door
handle

Wheel
arch

Wheel
hub

Treaded
tyre

Front passenger
lock casing

Headlamp
casing

Nearside front
wing

Light
diffusing
glass

Lightbulb

Chrome
housing

Securing
bracket

Exhausting system

In an engine, the gas and air mixture is sucked into the cylinder through inlet valves. The exhaust fumes are pushed out through exhaust valves. The *Traction Avant* engine had valves on top of the engine, whereas most cars of the time had valves at the side.

Willys Jeep

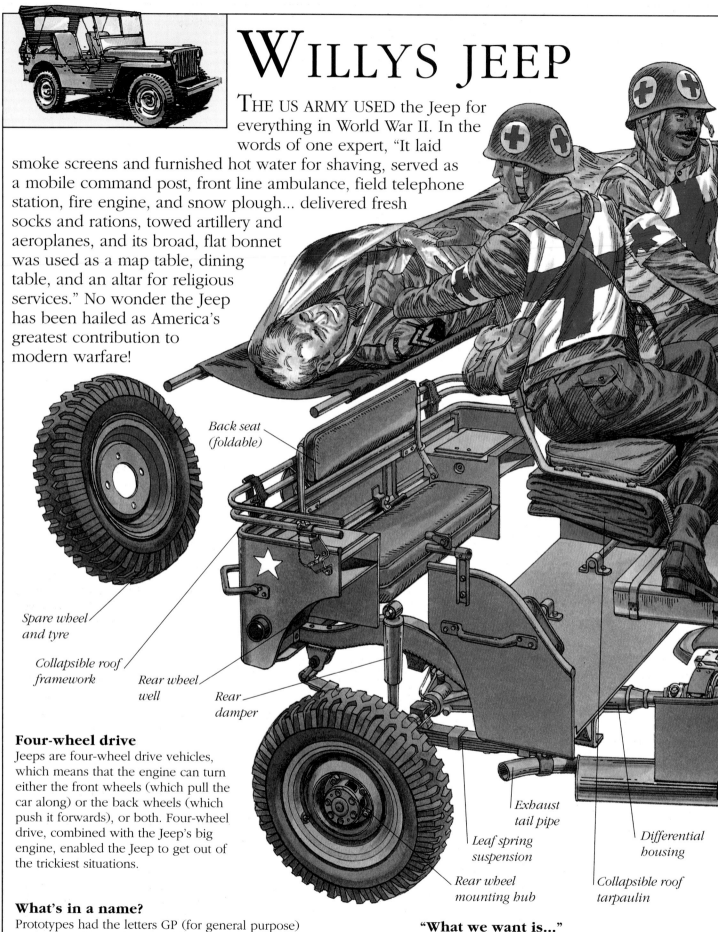

THE US ARMY USED the Jeep for everything in World War II. In the words of one expert, "It laid smoke screens and furnished hot water for shaving, served as a mobile command post, front line ambulance, field telephone station, fire engine, and snow plough... delivered fresh socks and rations, towed artillery and aeroplanes, and its broad, flat bonnet was used as a map table, dining table, and an altar for religious services." No wonder the Jeep has been hailed as America's greatest contribution to modern warfare!

Back seat (foldable)

Spare wheel and tyre

Collapsible roof framework

Rear wheel well

Rear damper

Exhaust tail pipe

Leaf spring suspension

Differential housing

Rear wheel mounting hub

Collapsible roof tarpaulin

Four-wheel drive
Jeeps are four-wheel drive vehicles, which means that the engine can turn either the front wheels (which pull the car along) or the back wheels (which push it forwards), or both. Four-wheel drive, combined with the Jeep's big engine, enabled the Jeep to get out of the trickiest situations.

What's in a name?
Prototypes had the letters GP (for general purpose) painted on their sides. Early models were given names such as "Bug", "Blitz Buggy", "Peep", "Midget", "Quack", and "Quad", but when one GI saw the letters GP, he ran them together and coined the name "Jeep". It stuck.

"What we want is..."
When they ordered the truck that became the Jeep, American military authorities specified a vehicle able to ford water, drive up a 45-degree slope and down a 35-degree one.

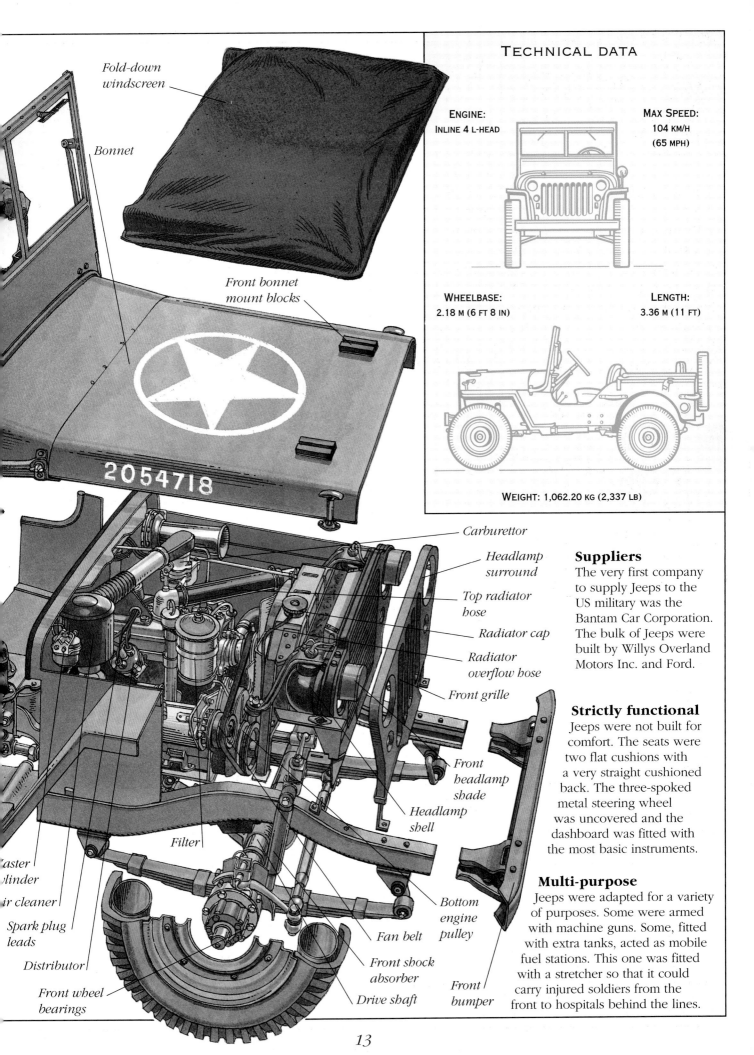

Fold-down
windscreen

Bonnet

Front bonnet
mount blocks

2054718

ENGINE:
INLINE 4 L-HEAD

MAX SPEED:
104 KM/H
(65 MPH)

WHEELBASE:
2.18 M (6 FT 8 IN)

LENGTH:
3.36 M (11 FT)

WEIGHT: 1,062.20 KG (2,337 LB)

Carburettor

Headlamp
surround

Top radiator
hose

Radiator cap

Radiator
overflow hose

Front grille

Front
headlamp
shade

Headlamp
shell

Bottom
engine
pulley

Fan belt

Front
bumper

Front shock
absorber

Drive shaft

Filter

...aster
...ylinder

...ir cleaner

Spark plug
leads

Distributor

Front wheel
bearings

Suppliers
The very first company
to supply Jeeps to the
US military was the
Bantam Car Corporation.
The bulk of Jeeps were
built by Willys Overland
Motors Inc. and Ford.

Strictly functional
Jeeps were not built for
comfort. The seats were
two flat cushions with
a very straight cushioned
back. The three-spoked
metal steering wheel
was uncovered and the
dashboard was fitted with
the most basic instruments.

Multi-purpose
Jeeps were adapted for a variety
of purposes. Some were armed
with machine guns. Some, fitted
with extra tanks, acted as mobile
fuel stations. This one was fitted
with a stretcher so that it could
carry injured soldiers from the
front to hospitals behind the lines.

BEETLE

VOLKS = PEOPLE'S. *WAGEN* = CAR. HENCE *VOLKSWAGEN*. When this popular little car was launched someone said it looked like a beetle – and the name stuck. It was developed because the German dictator, Adolf Hitler, decided that every German needed a car. The man he chose to design it was Ferdinand Porsche. His brief was simple: a small car, cheap to run, and able to carry a family of four or five, with a cruising speed of 100 km/h (62.5 mph) and priced below 1,000 reichsmarks (£150 at today's value). A few handmade models were built for Nazi VIPs before the war, and between 1939 and 1945 only military VWs were built. Production at the Wolfsburg factory started in earnest after 1945: the rest is history. Over 20 million Beetles were produced. No other car was ever in production for so long. The basic car shape was essentially the same throughout its life.

Sorry, you'll have to wait
Hitler decreed that people who wanted to buy a Volkswagen had to collect weekly savings stamps in advance. The war dashed any hopes that civilians may have had to own a VW. When it was over, the company agreed to honour stamps that had been bought before 1939.

Rear engine
Unlike most cars, the Volkswagen has its engine at the back and its luggage space is at the front. Inside a car engine there are metal tubes called cylinders. Combustion chambers, where the fuel and air are burned, are inside. The Volkswagen engine has four cylinders.

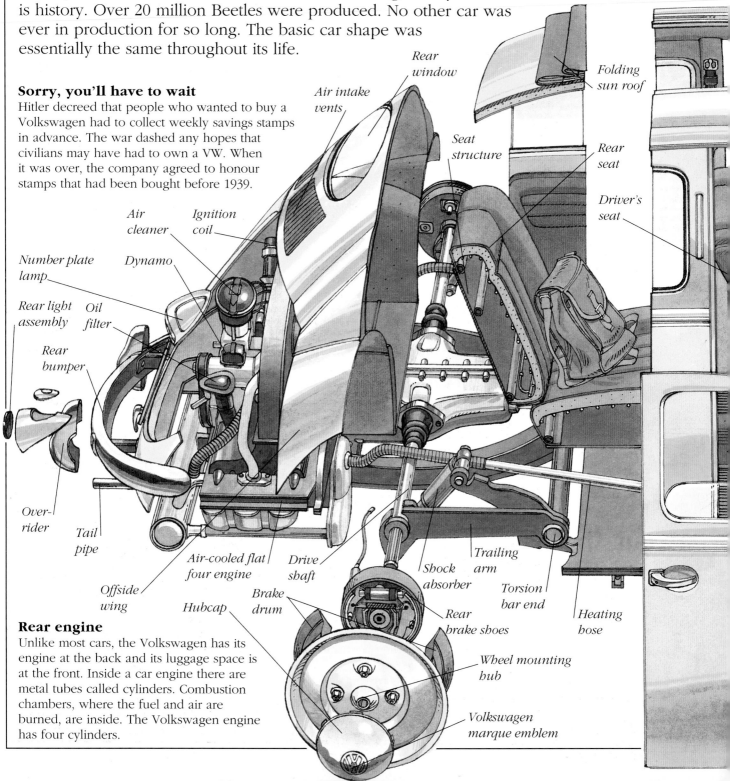

Rear window

Air intake vents

Folding sun roof

Seat structure

Rear seat

Driver's seat

Air cleaner

Ignition coil

Number plate lamp

Dynamo

Rear light assembly

Oil filter

Rear bumper

Over-rider

Tail pipe

Offside wing

Air-cooled flat four engine

Drive shaft

Brake drum

Hubcap

Shock absorber

Trailing arm

Rear brake shoes

Torsion bar end

Heating hose

Wheel mounting hub

Volkswagen marque emblem

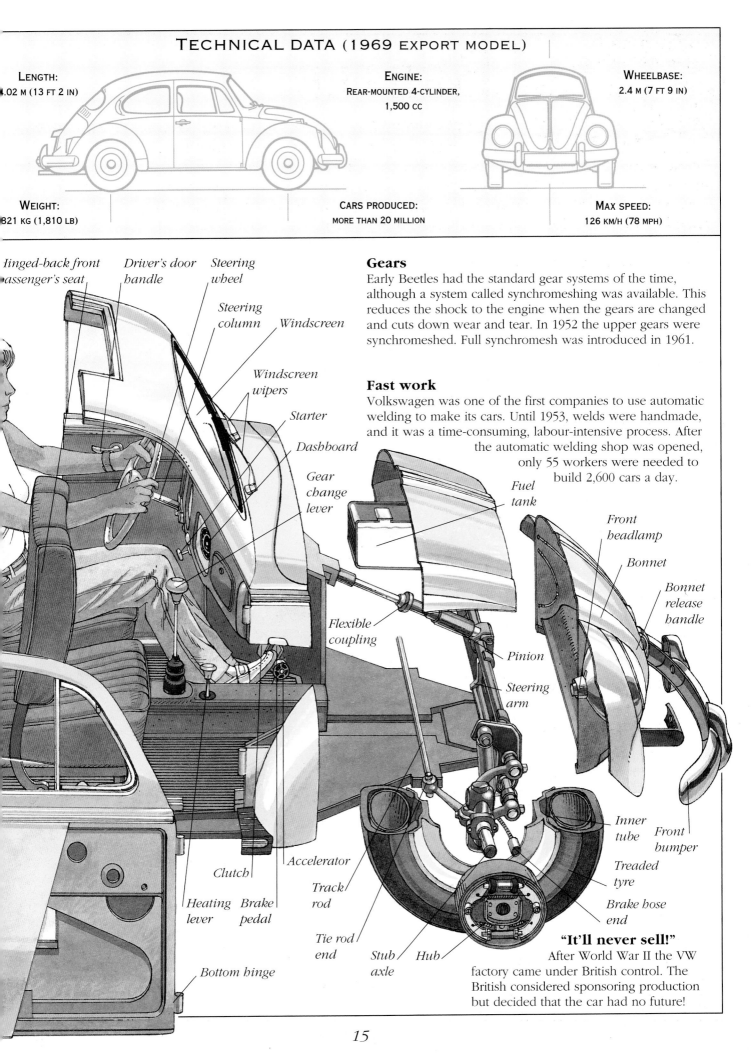

LENGTH:
4.02 M (13 FT 2 IN)

ENGINE:
REAR-MOUNTED 4-CYLINDER,
1,500 CC

WHEELBASE:
2.4 M (7 FT 9 IN)

WEIGHT:
821 KG (1,810 LB)

CARS PRODUCED:
MORE THAN 20 MILLION

MAX SPEED:
126 KM/H (78 MPH)

Gears

Early Beetles had the standard gear systems of the time, although a system called synchromeshing was available. This reduces the shock to the engine when the gears are changed and cuts down wear and tear. In 1952 the upper gears were synchromeshed. Full synchromesh was introduced in 1961.

Fast work

Volkswagen was one of the first companies to use automatic welding to make its cars. Until 1953, welds were handmade, and it was a time-consuming, labour-intensive process. After the automatic welding shop was opened, only 55 workers were needed to build 2,600 cars a day.

"It'll never sell!"

After World War II the VW factory came under British control. The British considered sponsoring production but decided that the car had no future!

15

GULLWING

IN 1952, THE CHAIRMAN of the German Daimler-Benz company wanted to show the world that his company was back in business after World War II. The car to do this was the new 300SL (Sports Light). SLs came second and fourth in the 1952 Mille Miglia road race, and won Le Mans and the Carrera Panamericana in the same year. Mercedes-Benz had no plans to build production models until an American car importer ordered 1,000 cars. The car was unveiled at the 1954 New York Auto Show where it caused a sensation. Today, it still does!

Gullwing doors
The doors were hinged along the top and opened upwards. This gave the car the nickname "Gullwing". But if the driver parked too close to a wall the door on that side could not be opened because of the huge arc it needed to swing upwards.

Gone but not forgotten
In mid-1957, the Gullwing was replaced by the 300SL roadster with a frame designed for conventional doors. In all 1,440 Gullwings and 1,858 roadsters were made.

Light or heavy
The racing sports model had a light metal alloy body, hence the designation SL, "Sports Light". This was not heavy enough for road models, which were built in much tougher steel, apart from the bonnet, doors, and boot lid.

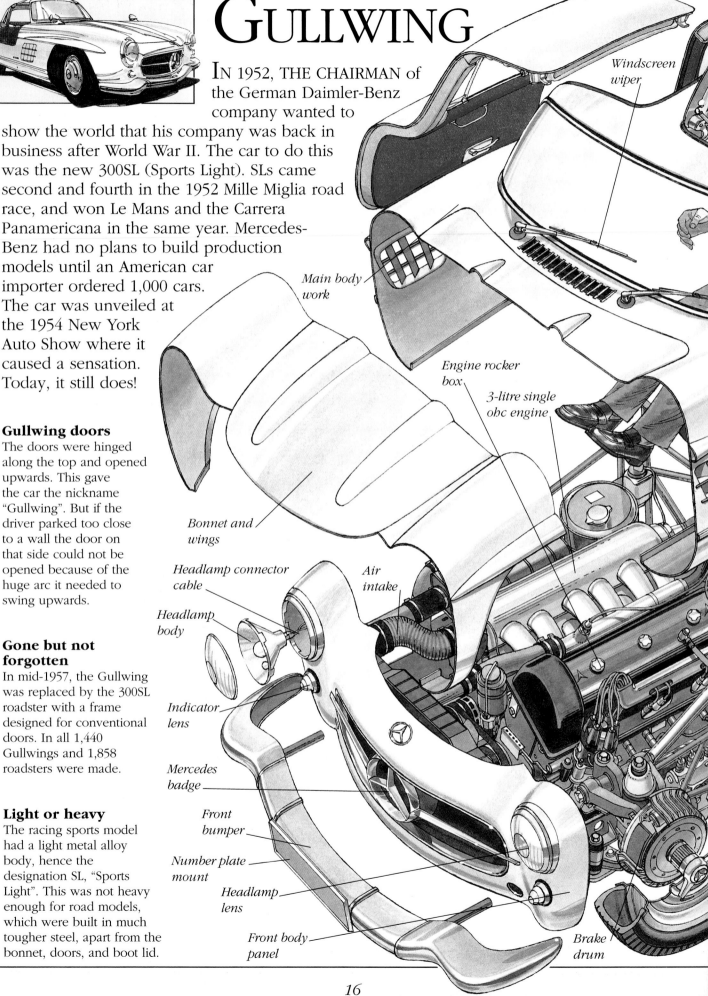

Windscreen wiper

Main body work

Engine rocker box

3-litre single ohc engine

Bonnet and wings

Headlamp connector cable

Headlamp body

Air intake

Indicator lens

Mercedes badge

Front bumper

Number plate mount

Headlamp lens

Front body panel

Brake drum

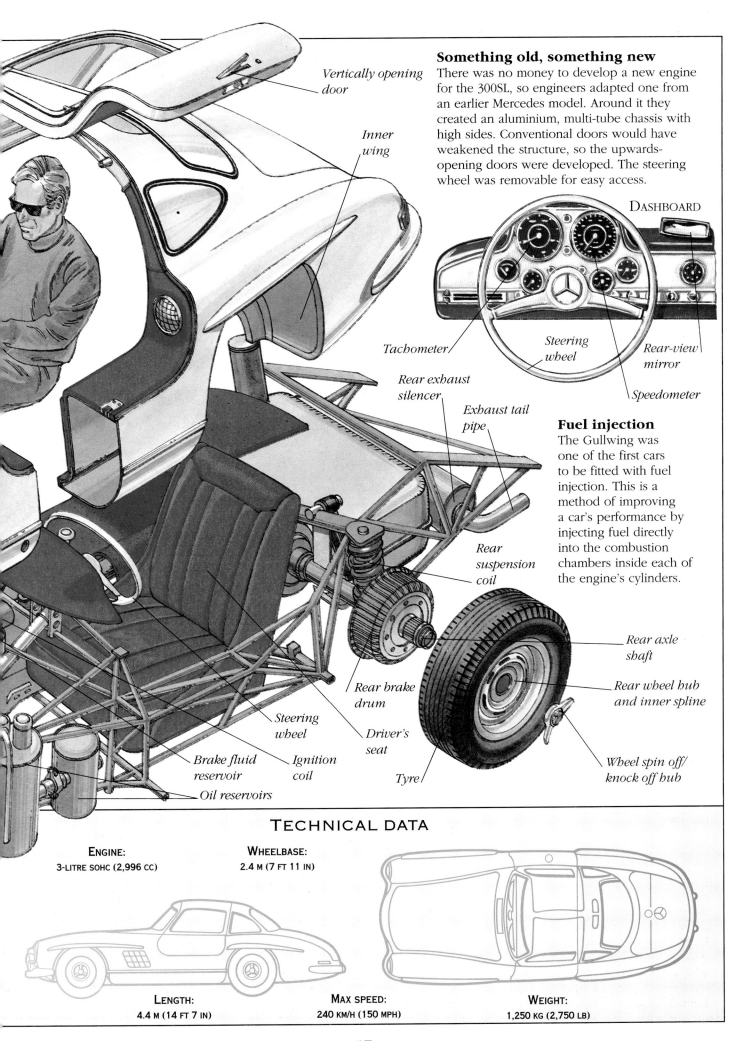

Vertically opening door

Inner wing

Something old, something new
There was no money to develop a new engine for the 300SL, so engineers adapted one from an earlier Mercedes model. Around it they created an aluminium, multi-tube chassis with high sides. Conventional doors would have weakened the structure, so the upwards-opening doors were developed. The steering wheel was removable for easy access.

DASHBOARD

Tachometer

Steering wheel

Rear-view mirror

Speedometer

Rear exhaust silencer

Exhaust tail pipe

Fuel injection
The Gullwing was one of the first cars to be fitted with fuel injection. This is a method of improving a car's performance by injecting fuel directly into the combustion chambers inside each of the engine's cylinders.

Rear suspension coil

Rear axle shaft

Rear wheel hub and inner spline

Rear brake drum

Steering wheel

Driver's seat

Brake fluid reservoir

Ignition coil

Tyre

Wheel spin off/ knock off hub

Oil reservoirs

TECHNICAL DATA

ENGINE:
3-LITRE SOHC (2,996 CC)

WHEELBASE:
2.4 M (7 FT 11 IN)

LENGTH:
4.4 M (14 FT 7 IN)

MAX SPEED:
240 KM/H (150 MPH)

WEIGHT:
1,250 KG (2,750 LB)

CADILLAC

CADILLAC HAVE BEEN MAKING CARS SINCE 1902, and it is the dream of millions of Americans to own one. To sit behind the wheel of a Cadillac is to tell the world that you are rich and successful, or have rich and successful parents! Cadillac has always taken the styles, taste, and mood of the day into account when designing its cars. In the 1950s, the cars were as bright and brassy as the rock 'n roll music that blared from their radios. Two of the great, glitzy gas-guzzlers of these days were the 1957 Sedan de Ville and Coupe de Ville. They were about 6 m (18 ft) long with extravagant tail fins, gleaming bumpers and grilles, and snappy sideflashes.

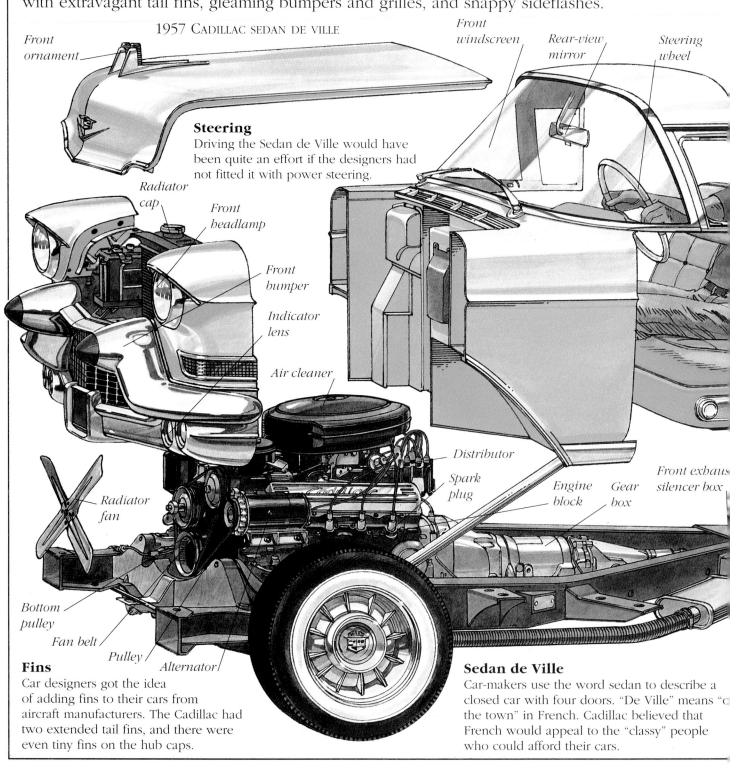

1957 CADILLAC SEDAN DE VILLE

Front ornament

Front windscreen

Rear-view mirror

Steering wheel

Steering
Driving the Sedan de Ville would have been quite an effort if the designers had not fitted it with power steering.

Radiator cap

Front headlamp

Front bumper

Indicator lens

Air cleaner

Distributor

Spark plug

Engine block

Gear box

Front exhaust silencer box

Radiator fan

Bottom pulley

Fan belt

Pulley

Alternator

Fins
Car designers got the idea of adding fins to their cars from aircraft manufacturers. The Cadillac had two extended tail fins, and there were even tiny fins on the hub caps.

Sedan de Ville
Car-makers use the word sedan to describe a closed car with four doors. "De Ville" means "of the town" in French. Cadillac believed that French would appeal to the "classy" people who could afford their cars.

TECHNICAL DATA (1957 2-DOOR COUPE DE VILLE)

LENGTH:
5.5 M (18 FT 4 IN)

MAX SPEED:
182 KM/H (113 MPH)

WHEELBASE:
3.3 M (10 FT 8 IN)

ENGINE:
300 BHP V8

WEIGHT:
2,084 KG (4,595 LB)

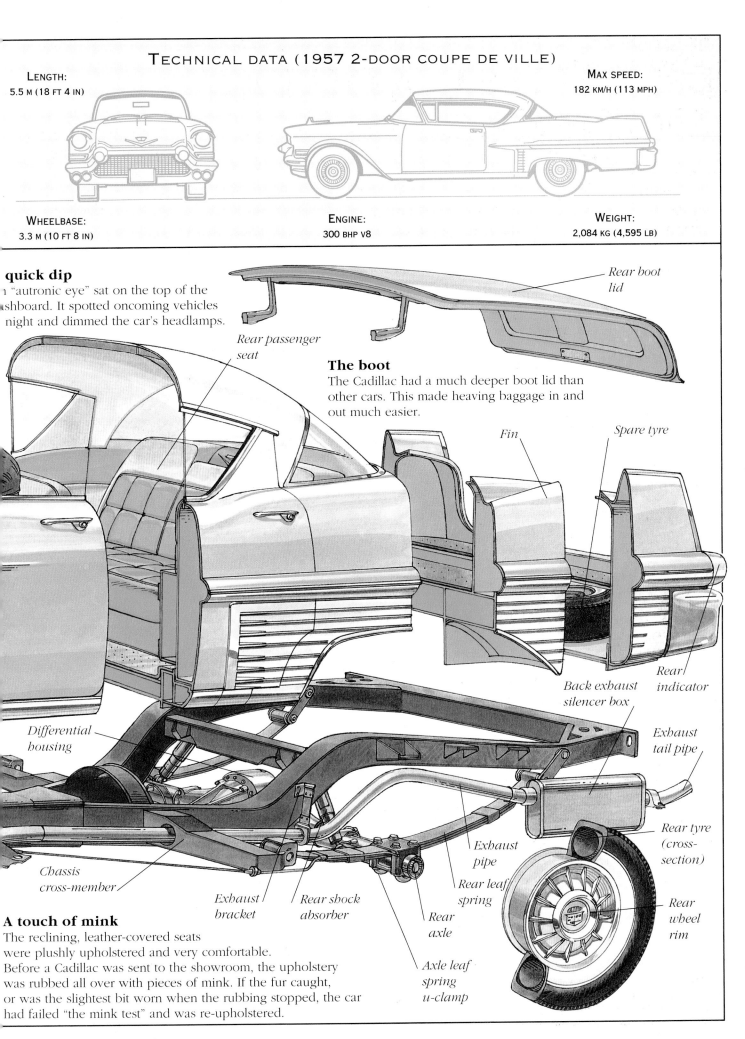

quick dip

n "autronic eye" sat on the top of the
shboard. It spotted oncoming vehicles
night and dimmed the car's headlamps.

Rear passenger seat

Rear boot lid

The boot
The Cadillac had a much deeper boot lid than
other cars. This made heaving baggage in and
out much easier.

Fin

Spare tyre

Rear indicator

Back exhaust silencer box

Exhaust tail pipe

Differential housing

Chassis cross-member

Exhaust bracket

Rear shock absorber

Rear axle

Exhaust pipe

Rear leaf spring

Axle leaf spring u-clamp

Rear tyre (cross-section)

Rear wheel rim

A touch of mink
The reclining, leather-covered seats
were plushly upholstered and very comfortable.
Before a Cadillac was sent to the showroom, the upholstery
was rubbed all over with pieces of mink. If the fur caught,
or was the slightest bit worn when the rubbing stopped, the car
had failed "the mink test" and was re-upholstered.

AUSTIN MINI

IN 1957, ALEX ISSIGONIS, head designer at the British Motor Corporation, was asked by BMC to design the smallest possible car capable of carrying four people. Two years later, the Mini was unveiled. At first, few people took the car seriously. But when it became obvious that the Mini was roomy, efficient, and cheap to run, sales soared. In 1986, the five-millionth Mini rolled off the production line.

Wheels
A small car needs small wheels. Large ones would have required wheel arches that used up too much passenger space. Issigonis decided to use 25.4-cm (10-in) wheels with a wheel rim of 8.9 cm (about 3 in). No company had ever produced tyres of this size. Fortunately, one tyre company, Dunlop, agreed to develop them.

The Mini Cooper
In 1961, BMC built the Mini Cooper, a version with a 997 cc engine. It was a huge success at racing circuits and rallies. In 1965, Paddy Hopkirk and Henry Liddon won the Monte Carlo Rally in a Cooper. During a hair-raising journey across Europe they lost their way, came into the gunsights of a Russian soldier, and were stopped by French police.

The engine
The prototype Mini, affectionately known as "The Orange Box", was fitted with a 948 cc engine. This gave it a top speed of 136 km/h (85 mph).

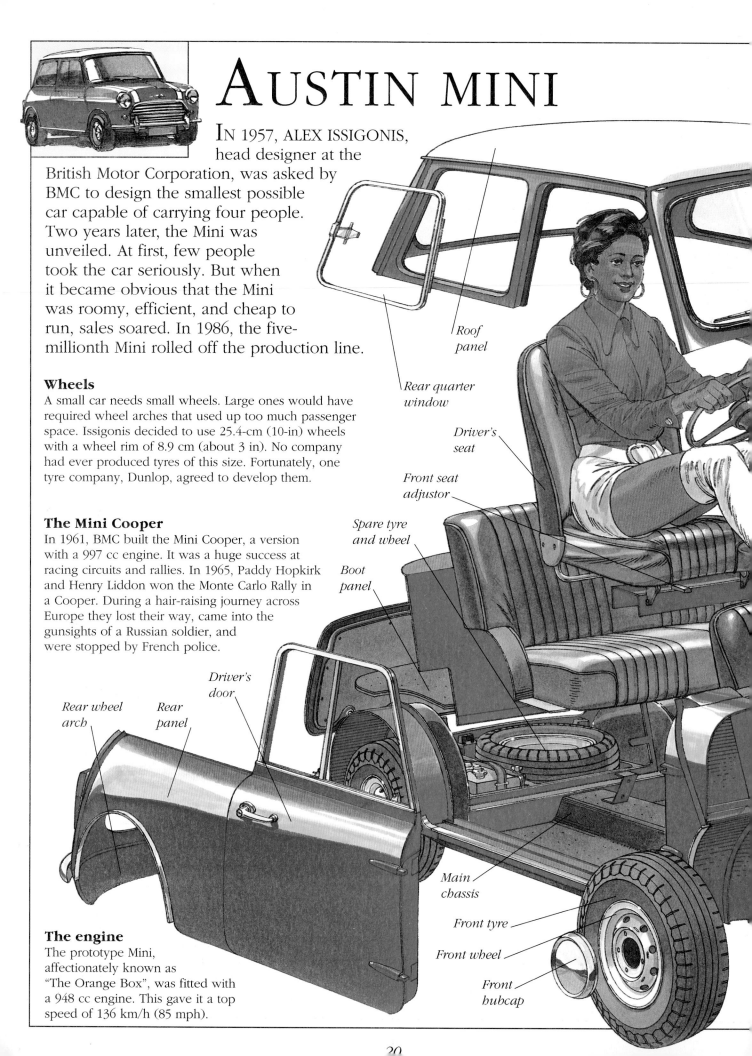

Roof panel

Rear quarter window

Driver's seat

Front seat adjustor

Spare tyre and wheel

Boot panel

Driver's door

Rear wheel arch

Rear panel

Main chassis

Front tyre

Front wheel

Front hubcap

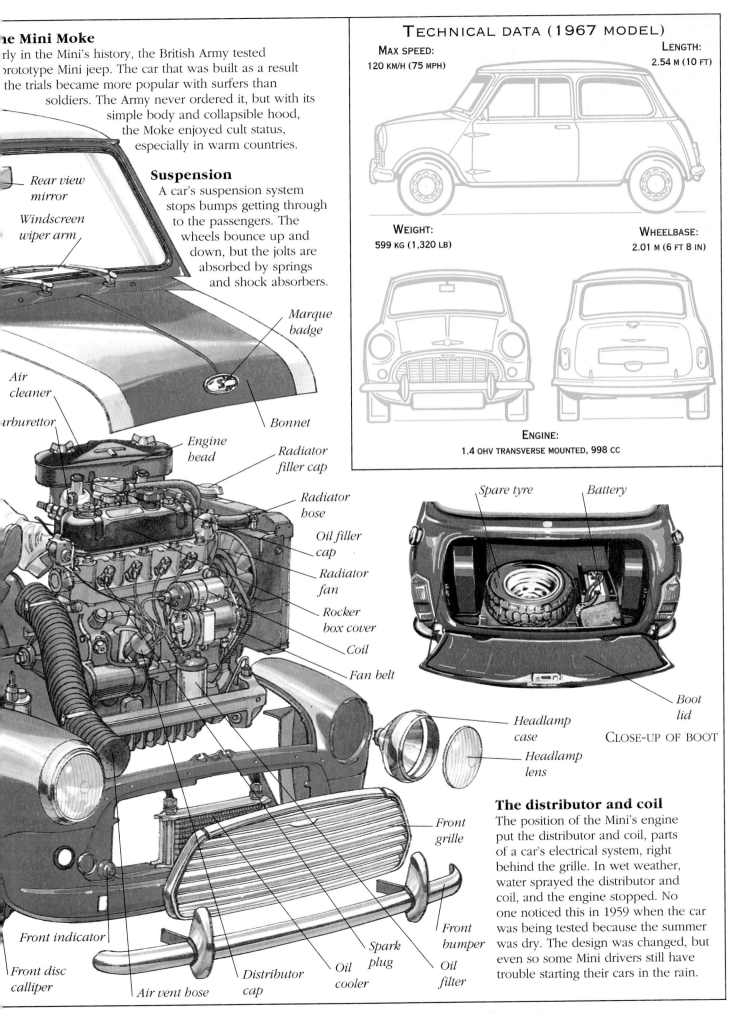

The Mini Moke

Early in the Mini's history, the British Army tested a prototype Mini jeep. The car that was built as a result of the trials became more popular with surfers than soldiers. The Army never ordered it, but with its simple body and collapsible hood, the Moke enjoyed cult status, especially in warm countries.

Suspension

A car's suspension system stops bumps getting through to the passengers. The wheels bounce up and down, but the jolts are absorbed by springs and shock absorbers.

Rear view mirror

Windscreen wiper arm

Air cleaner

Carburettor

Marque badge

Bonnet

Engine head

Radiator filler cap

Radiator hose

Oil filler cap

Radiator fan

Rocker box cover

Coil

Fan belt

Front indicator

Front disc calliper

Air vent hose

Distributor cap

Oil cooler

Spark plug

Oil filter

Front grille

Front bumper

TECHNICAL DATA (1967 MODEL)

MAX SPEED:
120 KM/H (75 MPH)

LENGTH:
2.54 M (10 FT)

WEIGHT:
599 KG (1,320 LB)

WHEELBASE:
2.01 M (6 FT 8 IN)

ENGINE:
1.4 OHV TRANSVERSE MOUNTED, 998 CC

Spare tyre

Battery

Boot lid

CLOSE-UP OF BOOT

Headlamp case

Headlamp lens

The distributor and coil

The position of the Mini's engine put the distributor and coil, parts of a car's electrical system, right behind the grille. In wet weather, water sprayed the distributor and coil, and the engine stopped. No one noticed this in 1959 when the car was being tested because the summer was dry. The design was changed, but even so some Mini drivers still have trouble starting their cars in the rain.

21

RALLY CAR

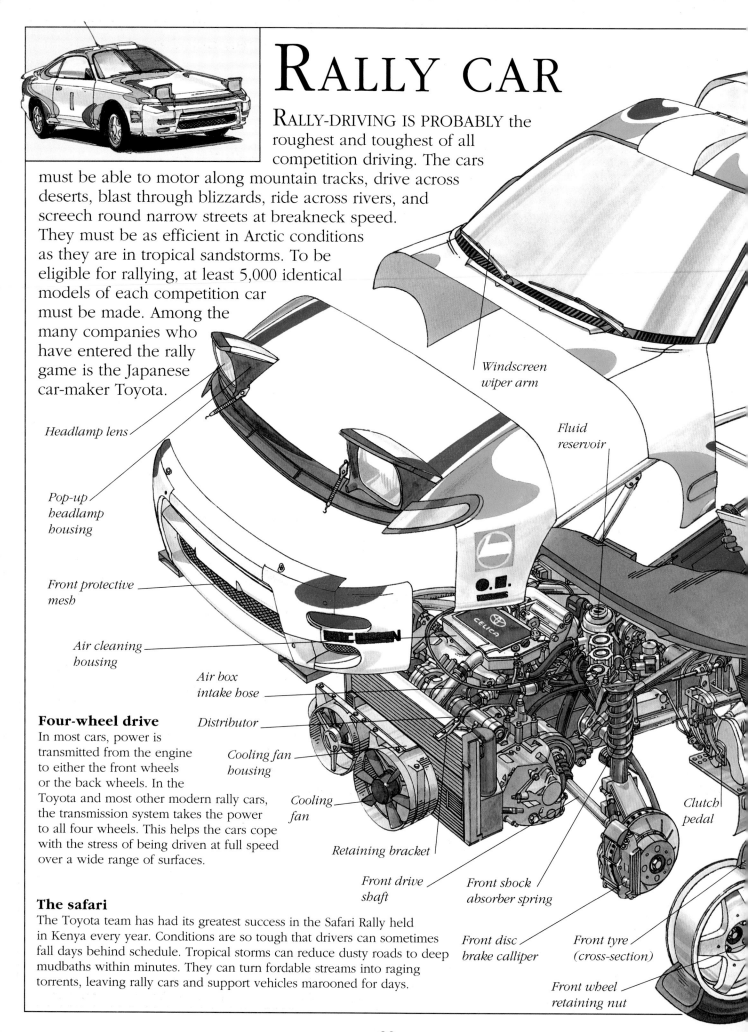

RALLY-DRIVING IS PROBABLY the roughest and toughest of all competition driving. The cars must be able to motor along mountain tracks, drive across deserts, blast through blizzards, ride across rivers, and screech round narrow streets at breakneck speed. They must be as efficient in Arctic conditions as they are in tropical sandstorms. To be eligible for rallying, at least 5,000 identical models of each competition car must be made. Among the many companies who have entered the rally game is the Japanese car-maker Toyota.

Headlamp lens

Pop-up headlamp housing

Front protective mesh

Air cleaning housing

Air box intake hose

Distributor

Cooling fan housing

Cooling fan

Retaining bracket

Front drive shaft

Windscreen wiper arm

Fluid reservoir

Clutch pedal

Front shock absorber spring

Front disc brake calliper

Front tyre (cross-section)

Front wheel retaining nut

Four-wheel drive

In most cars, power is transmitted from the engine to either the front wheels or the back wheels. In the Toyota and most other modern rally cars, the transmission system takes the power to all four wheels. This helps the cars cope with the stress of being driven at full speed over a wide range of surfaces.

The safari

The Toyota team has had its greatest success in the Safari Rally held in Kenya every year. Conditions are so tough that drivers can sometimes fall days behind schedule. Tropical storms can reduce dusty roads to deep mudbaths within minutes. They can turn fordable streams into raging torrents, leaving rally cars and support vehicles marooned for days.

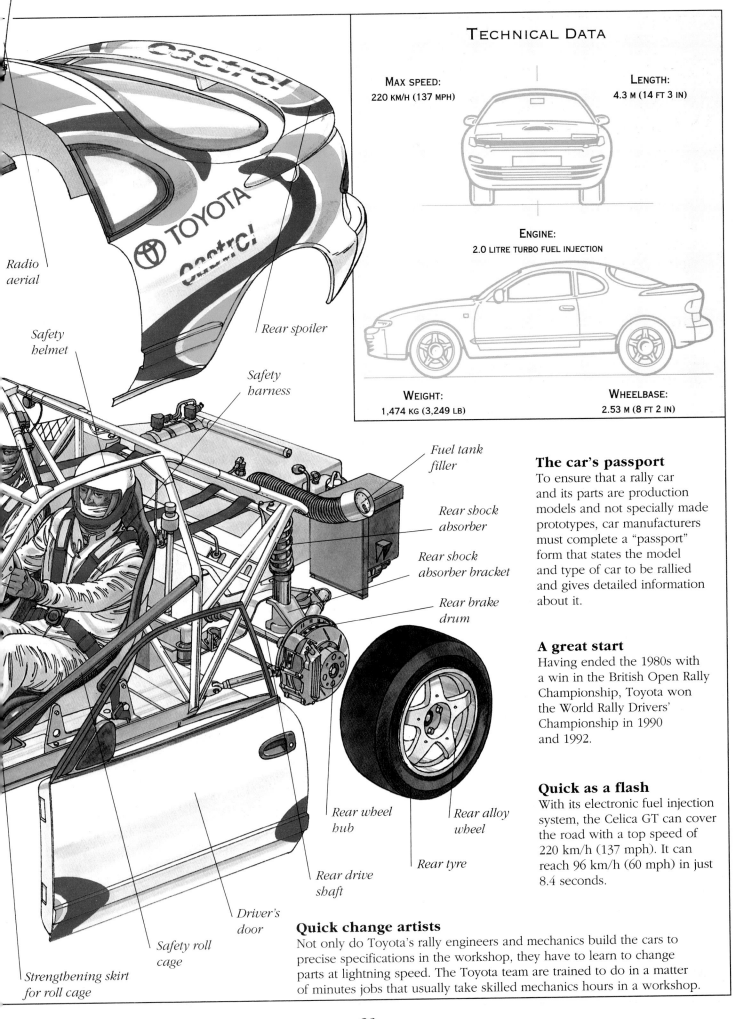

Radio aerial

Rear spoiler

Safety helmet

Safety harness

MAX SPEED:
220 KM/H (137 MPH)

LENGTH:
4.3 M (14 FT 3 IN)

ENGINE:
2.0 LITRE TURBO FUEL INJECTION

WEIGHT:
1,474 KG (3,249 LB)

WHEELBASE:
2.53 M (8 FT 2 IN)

Fuel tank filler

Rear shock absorber

Rear shock absorber bracket

Rear brake drum

Rear wheel hub

Rear alloy wheel

Rear tyre

Rear drive shaft

Driver's door

Safety roll cage

Strengthening skirt for roll cage

The car's passport

To ensure that a rally car and its parts are production models and not specially made prototypes, car manufacturers must complete a "passport" form that states the model and type of car to be rallied and gives detailed information about it.

A great start

Having ended the 1980s with a win in the British Open Rally Championship, Toyota won the World Rally Drivers' Championship in 1990 and 1992.

Quick as a flash

With its electronic fuel injection system, the Celica GT can cover the road with a top speed of 220 km/h (137 mph). It can reach 96 km/h (60 mph) in just 8.4 seconds.

Quick change artists

Not only do Toyota's rally engineers and mechanics build the cars to precise specifications in the workshop, they have to learn to change parts at lightning speed. The Toyota team are trained to do in a matter of minutes jobs that usually take skilled mechanics hours in a workshop.

FERRARI

IN 11.2 SECONDS A FERRARI *TESTAROSSA* can go from 0 to 160 km/h (100 mph). A few seconds later, it can reach its official top speed of 289.6 km/h (181 mph) – well over 2.5 times the speed limit in most countries of the world! The speedometer reads up to 320 km/h (200 mph). The *Testa Rossi* (Red Head) was one of the most successful racing cars of the 1960s and 1970s, so when Ferrari produced a top of the range road car, they decided to recall their glory days on the race circuit. In October 1984, a vivid red streamlined *Testarossa* drew gasps of admiration at the Paris Motor Show. In mid-1985 a new *Testarossa* cost £62,666. By 1994 the price had almost doubled, and with production limited to 4,000 a year, there is a waiting list of up to three years.

FERRARI LOGO ON WHEEL

Instrument binnacle

Windscreen

Steering wheel

Wing mirror

Luggage compartment

Aluminium bonnet

Star car
Perhaps the most famous *Testarossa* is the white one that starred in the TV series *Miami Vice*. When filming started, the makers used replicas. But Ferrari took them to court and soon the stars were behind the wheel of the real thing!

Spare tyre

Retractable headlamp unit

55W halogen headlamps

Glass-reinforced plastic bumper

High-speed gears
The *Testarossa* has five-speed gears. In first gear it has a maximum speed of 80.6 km/h (50.4 mph). That means it can go as fast in first gear as many cars go in top gear. The other gear speeds are just as impressive.

Gearshift control lever

Handbrake

Front suspension system

Brake disc caliper

Brake disc

Side slats

ENGINE:
FLAT-12 QUAD-CAM,
48 VALVE, 4,942 CC

MAX SPEED:
289.6 KM/H
(181 MPH)

LENGTH:
4.5 M (14 FT 8 IN)

WHEELBASE:
2.5 M (8 FT 5 IN)

WEIGHT:
1,670 KG (3,682 LB)

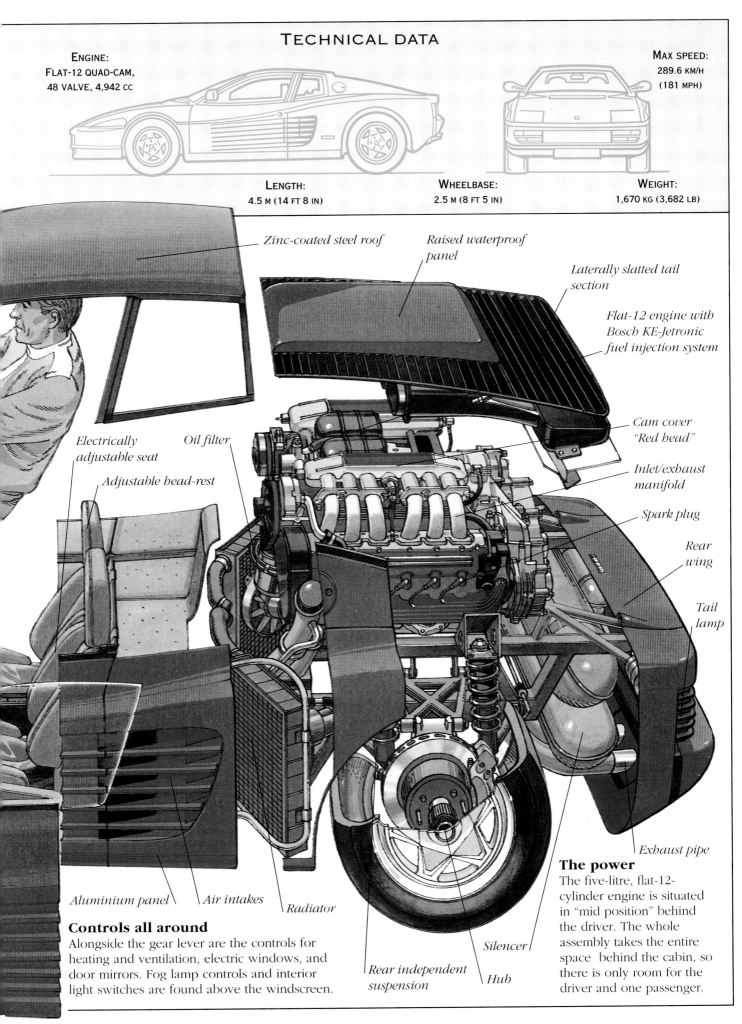

Zinc-coated steel roof

Raised waterproof panel

Laterally slatted tail section

Flat-12 engine with Bosch KE-Jetronic fuel injection system

Electrically adjustable seat

Oil filter

Adjustable head-rest

Cam cover "Red head"

Inlet/exhaust manifold

Spark plug

Rear wing

Tail lamp

Aluminium panel

Air intakes

Radiator

Silencer

Hub

Rear independent suspension

Exhaust pipe

Controls all around
Alongside the gear lever are the controls for heating and ventilation, electric windows, and door mirrors. Fog lamp controls and interior light switches are found above the windscreen.

The power
The five-litre, flat-12-cylinder engine is situated in "mid position" behind the driver. The whole assembly takes the entire space behind the cabin, so there is only room for the driver and one passenger.

FORMULA I

WHAT DOES THE LABEL STITCHED INTO THE BACK of a jumper have in common with a car roaring round a Grand Prix racetrack? They both bear the name Benetton! The Italian knitwear company first came into Grand Prix racing in 1983 when they started to sponsor the Tyrrell team, which was renamed Benetton-Tyrrell. In 1986 they went into Formula I racing in their own right with a car powered by a BMW engine. This was then replaced with one designed by Ford in association with Cosworth Engineering. In 1988 Grand Prixs were dominated by the McLaren-Honda team, but Benetton-Fords were placed in 12 of the season's 16 races. A major force had arrived in the world of motor racing.

Fastest lap
The 1988 Benetton-Ford clocked up the fastest lap in the German Grand Prix at the Hockenheim Circuit. With Alessandro Naninni at the wheel, the car ate up the 8.3-km (5.2-mile) circuit in 2.49 minutes. That's an average of 200 km/h (124.3 mph).

Real smoothies
If the track is dry, Grand Prix cars are fitted with treadless tyres called slicks. This allows a large area of the tyre to be on the track and makes the car more stable. Tyres with treads are used if it is wet. These give the car better grip.

Made in Britain
Benetton-Fords are made in a factory near the village of Enstone in Oxfordshire. The workshop looks more like an operating theatre than a car factory, with skilled technicians clad in white overalls and safety caps, working with the same precision as top surgeons. Building racing cars is expensive. The factory cost £12 million to set up.

On the wing
Formula I cars are fitted with two sets of wings or aerofoils, one low down at the front and another at the back. The car travels so fast that without these it could lift up off the track like an aeroplane. The aerofoils are designed so that the air rushes over them and pushes the car down to hold it on to the track.

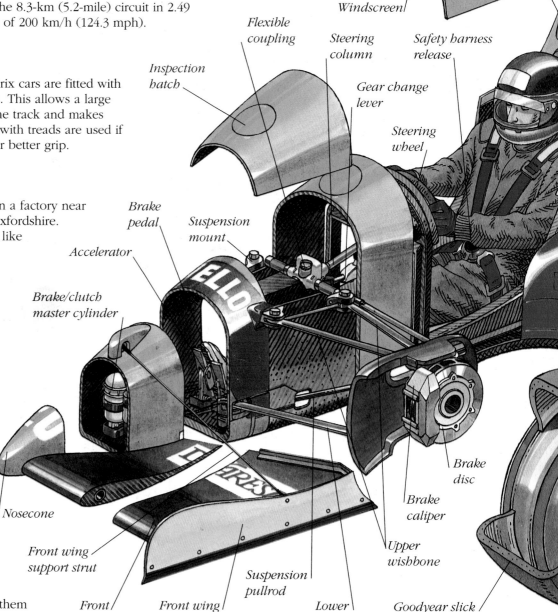

Rear-view mirror

Roll-over bar

Windscreen

Flexible coupling

Steering column

Safety harness release

Inspection hatch

Gear change lever

Steering wheel

Brake pedal

Suspension mount

Accelerator

Brake/clutch master cylinder

Nosecone

Front wing support strut

Front wing

Front wing endplate

Suspension pullrod

Lower wishbone

Upper wishbone

Brake disc

Brake caliper

Goodyear slick racing tyre

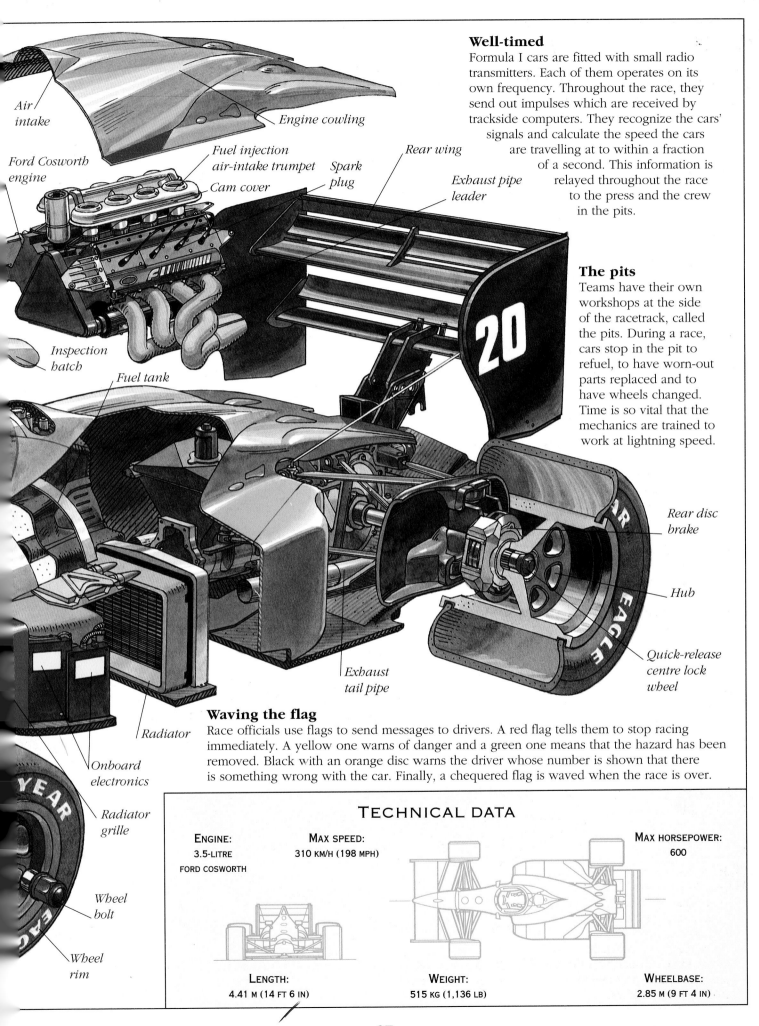

Air intake

Engine cowling

Ford Cosworth engine

Fuel injection air-intake trumpet

Cam cover

Spark plug

Rear wing

Exhaust pipe leader

Inspection hatch

Fuel tank

Radiator

Onboard electronics

Radiator grille

Wheel bolt

Wheel rim

Exhaust tail pipe

Rear disc brake

Hub

Quick-release centre lock wheel

Well-timed

Formula I cars are fitted with small radio transmitters. Each of them operates on its own frequency. Throughout the race, they send out impulses which are received by trackside computers. They recognize the cars' signals and calculate the speed the cars are travelling at to within a fraction of a second. This information is relayed throughout the race to the press and the crew in the pits.

The pits

Teams have their own workshops at the side of the racetrack, called the pits. During a race, cars stop in the pit to refuel, to have worn-out parts replaced and to have wheels changed. Time is so vital that the mechanics are trained to work at lightning speed.

Waving the flag

Race officials use flags to send messages to drivers. A red flag tells them to stop racing immediately. A yellow one warns of danger and a green one means that the hazard has been removed. Black with an orange disc warns the driver whose number is shown that there is something wrong with the car. Finally, a chequered flag is waved when the race is over.

TECHNICAL DATA

ENGINE:
3.5-LITRE
FORD COSWORTH

MAX SPEED:
310 KM/H (198 MPH)

MAX HORSEPOWER:
600

LENGTH:
4.41 M (14 FT 6 IN)

WEIGHT:
515 KG (1,136 LB)

WHEELBASE:
2.85 M (9 FT 4 IN)

CAR TIMELINE

THE STORY OF THE CAR BEGAN only slightly more than 100 years ago. Since that time, the automobile has evolved from a horse-drawn carriage lookalike to the aerodynamic, fuel-efficient shapes of today. Along the way, the car's basic design has acquired innovations such as supercharging, monocoque (one-piece) body construction, and front-wheel drive which have all contributed to the look and power of the modern late twentieth century automobile.

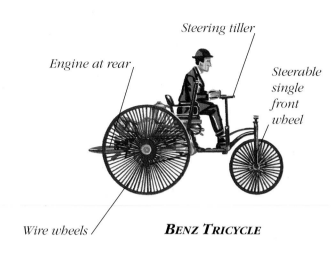

Steering tiller

Engine at rear

Steerable single front wheel

Wire wheels

BENZ TRICYCLE

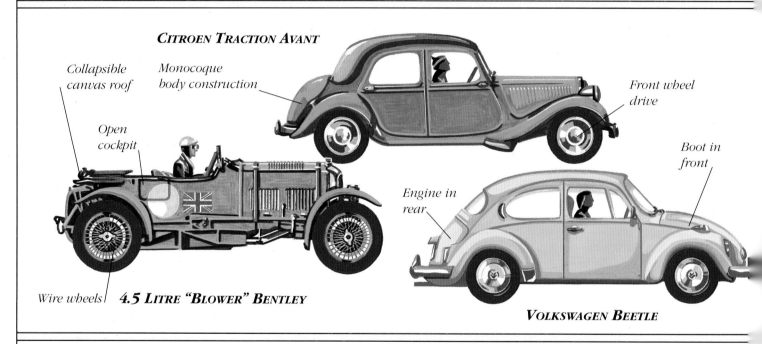

CITROEN TRACTION AVANT

Collapsible canvas roof

Monocoque body construction

Open cockpit

Front wheel drive

Boot in front

Engine in rear

Wire wheels   **4.5 LITRE "BLOWER" BENTLEY**

VOLKSWAGEN BEETLE

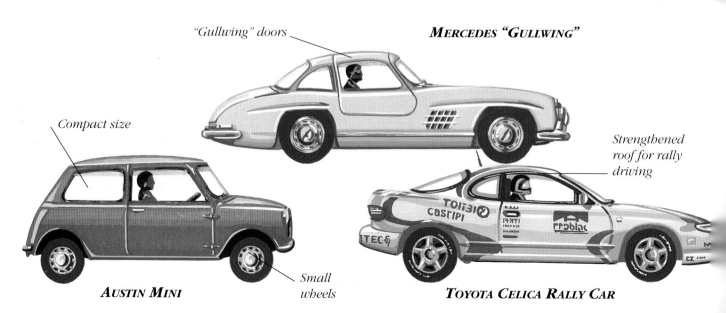

"Gullwing" doors

MERCEDES "GULLWING"

Compact size

Strengthened roof for rally driving

AUSTIN MINI

Small wheels

TOYOTA CELICA RALLY CAR

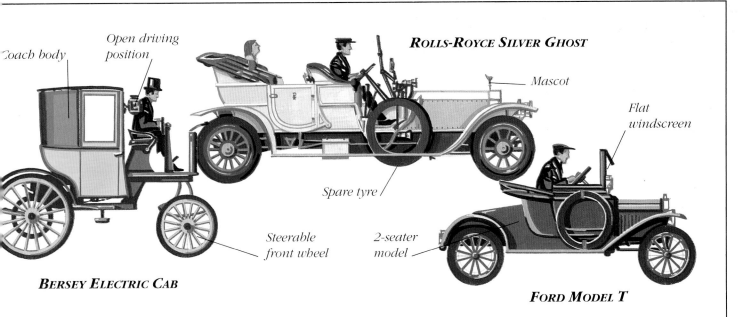

Coach body

Open driving position

ROLLS-ROYCE SILVER GHOST

Mascot

Flat windscreen

Spare tyre

Steerable front wheel

2-seater model

BERSEY ELECTRIC CAB

FORD MODEL T

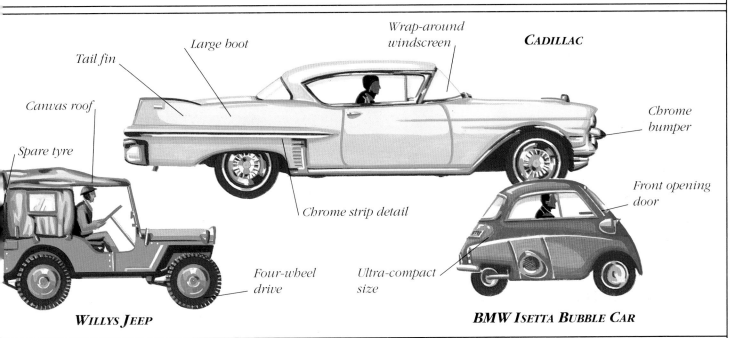

Wrap-around windscreen

CADILLAC

Large boot

Tail fin

Canvas roof

Chrome bumper

Spare tyre

Front opening door

Chrome strip detail

Four-wheel drive

Ultra-compact size

WILLYS JEEP

BMW ISETTA BUBBLE CAR

FERRARI "TESTAROSSA"

Aerodynamic shape cuts fuel consumption

Hatchback

Air intake

FIAT PUNTO

Rear spoiler

Front wing

FORMULA I RACING CAR

GLOSSARY

Accelerator pump
A device fitted to the carburettor to provide extra fuel to the fuel/air mixture when the accelerator pedal is pressed down.

Air cooling
A way of cooling the engine by using an engine-driven fan that forces cool air at high speed over the engine's surfaces.

Alternator
A device for turning rotating mechanical energy into electrical energy.

Ammeter
A device that measures the electrical current supplied to the battery by the alternator or drawn from the battery by the car's electrical system.

Antifreeze
A chemical added to the water in the cooling system to reduce the temperature at which it freezes.

Automatic transmission
A gearbox that selects the correct gear ratio when the car is moving according to the car's speed and load.

Axle
The spindle on which a wheel revolves.

Battery
The part of the car that supplies the power that works the lights, ignition, radio, and other parts of the car that function by electricity.

Bearing
A hard-wearing surface, usually metal, designed to reduce wear and friction when it moves another part.

Big end
The end of the connecting rod, attached to the crankshaft, that transmits the rod's movement to the crankshaft.

Brake caliper
Part of a disc brake, housing the brake pads and hydraulically operated pistons.

Brake disc
The rotating disc part of a brake system, clamped between friction pads.

Brake horse power (BHP)
A measure of the power needed to bring a moving body to a halt.

Brake pad
The friction material and metal backing-plate of a disc brake system.

Brake shoe
The friction material and the curved metal part of a drum brake system.

Brakes
The discs or drums that bring the car to a halt when they are put into contact with the wheels.

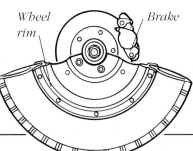

Wheel rim   *Brake*

Camshaft
The shaft driven by the crankshaft which operates the engine's valves.

Carburettor
The device that sprays a mixture of petrol and air into the cylinders.

Catalytic converter
Part of the exhaust system that cuts down the amount of harmful gases released into the air.

Chassis
The rigid frame on which the car's body is built up.

Choke
A device, used in cold weather when starting a car, which reduces the amount of air in the carburettor. This makes the fuel/air mixture easier to ignite.

Clutch
The pedal which when pressed disconnects the engine from the gearbox to enable the driver to change gear.

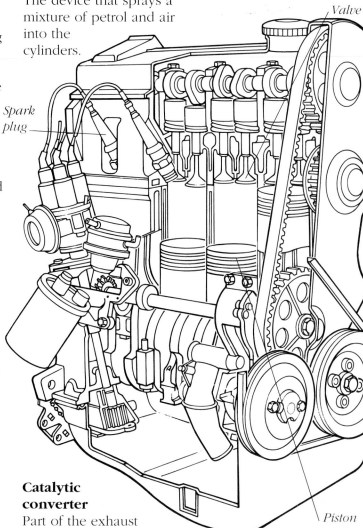

Valve

Spark plug

Piston

Combustion chamber
The part of the cylinder head where the fuel/air mixture is compressed by a piston and ignited by a spark.

Crankshaft
The shaft turned by the pistons which transmits power to the wheels.

Cylinder
The metal tube encasing a sliding piston.

Cylinder block
The part of the engine that contains the cylinders, crankshaft, and pistons.

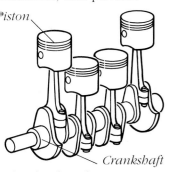

Piston

Crankshaft

Cylinder head
The part at the top of an engine where the valves are situated.

Dashboard
The strip of wood or metal facing the driver on which the instruments are fitted.

Diesel engine
An engine that runs on diesel oil rather than refined petrol.

Differential
The system of gears in the transmission system which enables the wheels to turn at different speeds when turning corners.

Disc brake
A brake with a rotating disc held by clamps between hydraulically operated friction pads.

Drum brake
A braking system whereby "shoes", lined with friction pads, run inside a cylindrical drum attached to the wheel.

Exhaust pipe
The metal tube along which fumes run from the engine to be expelled into the air.

Filter
A device for removing unwanted particles from air, oil, or fuel.

Fuel injection
A way of introducing fuel into the engine to increase performance.

Gear lever
The column which the driver moves after operating the clutch to change gear.

Gearbox
The part of the transmission system that provides the different gears that enable the car to be driven at different speeds.

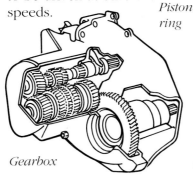

Gearbox

Horsepower
A measurement of power.

Hydraulics
The transmission of pressure through a fluid.

Ignition system
The electrical system made up of the battery, ignition coil, distributor, switch, spark plugs, and wiring that act to provide the spark that ignites the air/fuel mixture in the engine.

Independent suspension
A suspension system by which the movement of one wheel of a pair has no effect on the other.

Leaded petrol
Petrol with extra lead added to it during manufacture.

Piston
The metal part that fits tightly inside the cylinder and slides up and down to turn the crankshaft.

Piston ring
A strong metal ring that runs around a piston to ensure the tightest possible seal between the piston and the cylinder wall.

Piston ring

Piston

Securing pin

Power steering
A system that uses hydraulic fluid pressure supplied by an engine-driven pump to make the steering system more responsive to the touch.

Quarter light
The small triangular window fitted in front of the front window and behind the rear one.

Shock absorber
The part that cushions the bumps when a car is driven over an uneven surface.

Spark-ignition
The system whereby a spark produced by the spark plugs ignites the fuel/air mixture drawn in to the engine cylinders, thus providing the power to drive the engine.

Spark plug
The pair of electrodes, separated by a ceramic surface, that produces the spark in the spark-ignition system.

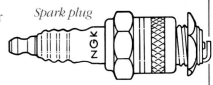

Spark plug

Suspension
The parts of the car that hold it over the wheels.

Synchromesh
Part of the gearbox that matches the speed of one gear with another to ensure smooth gear changes.

Tachometer
A device that measures the speed of the engine in revolutions per minute. Also known as the rev counter.

Torque
The turning force generated by a rotating part.

Unleaded petrol
Petrol which has natural lead content with no extra added in manufacture.

Valve
A device that opens to allow gas or fluid to flow through it, and closes to stop the flow.

Vee engine
An engine in which the cylinders are fitted in two banks which form a V-shape.

INDEX

Acknowledgements

Dorling Kindersley would like to thank the following people who helped in the preparation of this book:
Lynn Bresler for the index
Additional artworks by John See